GREAT MOMENTS IN BASEBALL

by Wayne R. Coffey

Watermill Press

Cover photo: Mickey Palmer/Focus on Sports

Inside photos: Wide World Photos

CONTENTS

GREAT
MOMENTS IN
BASEBALL

ROGER MARIS
HITS 61 HOME RUNS

In 1960 the Yankees made a trade with the Kansas City Athletics. New York sent Marv Thornberry, Hank Bauer, Norm Siebern, and Don Larsen to the A's in exchange for Joe DeMaestri, Kent Hadley, and a promising 26-year-old outfielder named Roger Maris. Neither DeMaestri nor Hadley figured much in the Yankees' continued dominance of the American League in the following seasons. But Roger Maris certainly did. All by himself, he made that swap one the A's would never forget.

Signed by the Cleveland Indians for a $5,000 bonus, Maris was hailed as "Cleveland's Mickey Mantle." He was a good bet for Rookie of the Year in 1957 before breaking two ribs while sliding and tailing off the latter part of the season. The next year, split between Cleveland and Kansas City, which parted with a talented first baseman named Vic Power to get him, Maris emerged as a bona fide slugger. He walloped 28 homers and collected 80 r.b.i.'s. He came out blazing in 1959, leading the league in batting in late July with a .344 average. But he slipped badly, a prolonged slump dropping him to .272 by season's end. His home-run output fell to 18.

Nobody disputed the fact that Roger had a great deal of potential. But his lack of consistency troubled the A's. That was one of the prime reasons they traded him to the Yanks, who were lured by the lefty swinger's power to right field, an asset perfectly suited to the short porch in Yankee Stadium.

The young outfielder may have had a hot-and-cold career to that point. But once he put on the Yankee pinstripes, Maris was all hot. He cracked 39 homers and walked off with the league's Most Valuable Player Award.

Maris started slowly in 1961. He hit only seven home runs by late May, and was batting around .240. But for the remaining four months of that season, Roger Maris went on a home-run rampage that became the biggest news in baseball. He commanded headlines in newspapers coast to coast. He was engulfed by a mob of reporters after every game. His day-by-day efforts were followed by millions, and he played out the season under a spotlight harsher than any a ballplayer has ever known. The reason for the fanfare was that Roger Maris challenged the most glamorous baseball record of them all—Babe Ruth's 60 home runs in one season.

Actually, the assault on the Babe's legendary mark was two-pronged, because teammate Mickey Mantle was also crashing fences at a record-breaking clip. In fact, before a severe infection and chronic knee problems limited Mickey's playing time late in the season, both he and Maris were on a historic course. The two sluggers each had 45 homers after just 108 games, 16 games ahead of Ruth's pace of 1927. Even with Mantle's misfortune, the dynamic duo finished with 115 home runs, making them the greatest long-ball tandem in baseball history.

The closer Roger got to the fabled 60, the more intense grew the pressure. The incessant questioning from the media grated on Maris, by nature an extremely private person. Life became uncomfortable for Roger, and at times nearly intolerable.

"Can you break Ruth's record?" "What would you rather do, hit .300 or break the record?" "Is winning the pennant more important to you than the record?" "Do you think you're hitting so many homers because of the livelier baseball?" The herd of reporters grew by the day, and the questions rarely changed and never stopped.

Maris responded by withdrawing even more. Often he was curt with reporters, sometimes even rude. Many of them showed little sensitivity to him; why, he thought, should he show any to them? Things got so bad toward the end of the chase that once Maris burst into tears during a meeting with the new Yankee manager, Ralph Houk. "I can't handle this," he said dejectedly. "They keep asking the same questions. It never lets up." Roger became so anxious that his hair began to fall out, a condition doctors attributed directly to nerves.

"I never wanted all this hoopla," said Maris. "All I wanted is to be a good ballplayer, hit 25 or 30 homers, drive in 100 runs, hit .280, and help my club win pennants. I just wanted to be one of the guys, an average ballplayer having a good season.''

But it wasn't to be. Roger Maris was *the* guy, and in spite of everything else, the home runs continued to jump off his bat. With 11 games to play, Maris had 58 round-trippers. The pressure on his sturdy shoulders became more excruciating, when Ford Frick, the commissioner, ruled that for Roger to be given credit for breaking Babe's record, he would have to do it in 154 games, which was the length of the schedule in Ruth's time. If Roger were to reach 60 or more after that 154th game, Frick said, the record would carry an asterisk next to it. The ruling incensed Roger, who felt the baseball establishment did not want some little-known outfielder upstaging the grandest figure in the game's history. ''Do you know any other records that have been broken since the 162-game schedule that have an asterisk?'' he posed. ''I don't. Frick decided on the asterisk after I had about 50 homers and it looked like I'd break Ruth's record.''

But the ruling held, so when the Yankees went to Baltimore, Maris needed two homers in three games to tie Ruth. The young slugger was stopped through the first two games. It came down to one game—No. 154. Facing a hard-throwing right-hander, Milt Pappas, Maris lined out to right in his first appearance. In the third, he stepped into a pitch and drove it some 380 feet, well over the right-field wall, for No. 59. He needed only one more.

In the fifth, Maris got hold of one and launched it deep to right, but it curved foul and he wound up striking out. In the seventh, he rocketed another long foul, then connected for a long fly that was hauled in just in front of the wall. Only one shot remained. He stepped in for his rips in the ninth inning. Now facing knuckle baller Hoyt Wilhelm, Roger waited for the fluttering pitch, tried to check his swing, but couldn't. He grounded softly to first base. "I gave it all I had," said Maris later. "But it wasn't enough. I'm glad it's over. The pressure is off."

Across the locker room, Mantle raved about Roger's performance that night, calling it "one of the greatest shows of power hitting" he had ever seen. Maris, after all, had hit one homer and four long drives which, with a little luck, could have landed in the seats. "He didn't have much luck," said Mickey, "but he had all the rest—skill and power and all the courage a man could want."

Eight games remained. Asterisk or no asterisk, the chase went on. After being held in check for three games, Roger Maris returned to Yankee Stadium. In the third inning, against a 22-year-old Oriole hurler named Jack Fisher, Maris lashed at a belt-high curve ball and crashed it into the upper deck. He had tied the Babe! The fans went wild, demanding that he come out of the dugout and take a bow. Reluctantly, he did, doffing his cap and waving to the jubilant throng. "I didn't know what to do," Roger said later. "I was never in a spot like that." Physically and mentally exhausted from the grueling schedule and the tension-packed quest for the record, Roger took a day off the next game. He

**The Maris Swing: Roger walloping the
record-breaker.**

had three left in which to set a new major-league home-run record. He was blanked in the first two. It all came down to one game—No. 162. The Boston Red Sox were the opponents, and Tracy Stallard, a fast-balling 24-year-old right-hander, was the pitcher.

In his first at bat, Maris connected well on an opposite-field drive, but the ball was caught in fairly deep left field. He got another turn in the fourth. Stallard threw a fast ball wide of the plate, then a curve low and in. The 25,154 fans at the Stadium had not come to see Roger passed. They booed loudly.

Maris banged his spikes clean with the end of his bat and dug in for the next offering. Stallard reared back and hummed one, high and out over the plate. Roger swung. *Crack!* The ball bolted off his bat, deep to right. Outfielder Lu Clinton went to the wall. He ran out of room. The ball carried into the lower right-field seats. Roger Maris had done it! The crowd went berserk, cheering wildly for the new home-run king. The ovation lasted five minutes, and again Roger was summoned from the dugout for a bow.

"It was the biggest home run I ever hit," exclaimed a relieved Roger in the champagne-soaked clubhouse. "I knew it was gone the minute I hit it. I can't explain how I felt. I don't know what I was thinking of as I rounded the bases. My mind was a blank.

"It's the greatest thrill I ever had. I thought nothing could match the thrill I got when I hit my 60th, but this beats everything.

"Whether I beat Ruth's record or not is for others to say," Maris went on. "But it gives me a wonderful feeling to know that I'm the only man in history to hit 61 home runs. Nobody can take that away from me. Babe Ruth was a big man in baseball, maybe the biggest ever. I'm not saying I am of his caliber, but I'm glad to say I hit more than he did in a season. I'd like to have done it in 154 games, but since I didn't, I'm glad now that I did it in 162 games."

Roger Maris never approached that number again. In fact, he never hit more than 33 homers in any season after that. Having shattered such a momentous record and having been given so much unwanted publicity, he became, in many ways, a victim of his one sensational season. He had some terrific years after that, but nothing he did ever seemed to be enough. He constantly feuded with the New York press; he felt many unfair things were written about him, and many reporters felt it was nearly impossible to deal with him. Frequently he got booed in Yankee Stadium, where his cardinal sin was to hit more homers than his good friend—and the fans' darling—Mickey Mantle.

Plagued by a string of injuries, Roger's production dwindled as the years passed. Finally, in 1966, with the once-awesome Yankee club a shadow of its former self, Roger Maris was traded to the St. Louis Cardinals. It was just as well; Roger was happy to be moving along. He played two years in St. Louis, and helped spark the Cards to back-to-back pennants.

The pressure of the chase shows on Roger's face.

At the relatively young age of 33, Roger Maris retired in 1968. It had been a turbulent career, and for much of it Roger seemed like a troubled man, a player who appeared to get little joy out of the game. But he also was a man of tremendous drive and courage who endured months of fierce pressure that perhaps no other ballplayer has ever known. What's more, he survived, and he succeeded. As he said on that historic day, October 1, 1961, "If I never hit another home run, this is one they can never take away from me."

NOLAN RYAN
PITCHES FIVE NO-HITTERS

"He's the only man in baseball I'm afraid of," said Reggie Jackson.

"If he ever hits me with a fast ball, I'll have him arrested for manslaughter," said Harmon Killebrew.

The two sluggers, who between them have belted nearly 1,000 home runs, were talking about Nolan Ryan—a long, lean Texan who has spent more than 15 years making life unpleasant for major-league batters. If a vote were taken on which pitcher hitters would least like to face, there's every chance Ryan would win going away.

The reason, simply stated, is Ryan's Express, the nickname given to Nolan's fast ball. Of course it's impossible to know for certain, but most long-time baseball observers agree that Ryan throws a baseball harder than anyone ever has. His fast ball has been timed at 100.9 miles per hour, the fastest ever recorded. If it can go 100 miles in only an hour, imagine how fast it can cover the 60 feet, six inches between home plate and the pitcher's mound.

For a time, it seemed that Ryan was too fast for

his own good. The problem was that neither he nor anyone else had any idea where his ball was going. First signed by the New York Mets, Nolan advanced to the majors at the tender age of 19 and was up to stay at 21. He showed flashes of brilliance in his four full seasons with the Mets; when he was on, he was untouchable. It was just that he wasn't on as often as the Mets would have liked. He was as wild and inconsistent as he was fast, much the way another fireballer, Sandy Koufax, was early in his career.

Finally, the Mets' patience grew thin. Deciding they no longer wanted to wait for the flame-throwing youngster to live up to his potential, they traded Nolan to the California Angels in 1971. In return, the Mets got Jim Fregosi, a former all-star whom they hoped would solve their chronic third-base woes. The Mets paid dearly for their impatience. It was the worst trade since the Indians surrendered Manhattan Island for $24. While Fregosi was rapidly proving he was over the hill, Nolan Ryan was quickly becoming king of it.

A regular starting pitcher for the first time, Nolan racked up 19 wins and struck out 329 batters in his maiden season with the Angels. He had his bouts with wildness, a problem he has never completely conquered, but he had matured into a more consistent hurler. His ERA was just 2.28, and by the time the season ended, a lot of American League hitters were wishing the Angels would trade him back to the Mets. Still only 25, Ryan, they knew, would only get better. And that meant nothing but trouble, as the Kansas City Royals found out early in 1973.

The Ryan Express.

Inning after inning, Ryan rifled through the Royals' order. Through five frames, Nolan did not yield a hit. The sixth and seventh came and went, and still the Royals were hitless. In the eighth, pinch hitter Gail Hopkins popped one to short left. It looked like trouble until shortstop Rudy Meoli darted back and made a running catch. It was into the ninth. Ryan was just three outs from every pitcher's dream—a no-hit game.

He got the first out on a foul pop, the second on a strikeout, his 12th of the game. Up stepped Amos Otis, a dangerous hitter. Ryan wheeled and offered, and Otis drove the ball to deep right center. Ken Berry raced back, and a few steps from the wall, snared the drive to end the game. Ryan had done it! A no-hitter! Afterward, John Mayberry, Kansas City's slugging first baseman, said, "He was throwing the ball harder than any man I ever saw."

"I felt terrible warming up," said Nolan later. "I didn't seem to have any stuff. I think I got stronger as the game went on, but I never really had exceptional stuff throughout."

Two months later to the day, Nolan took the hill in Detroit's Tiger Stadium. It has long been known as a hitter's ballpark, but there wasn't much hitting done that night—not by the Tigers, anyway. Ryan, blistering from his first pitch, whiffed 12 of the first 14 men he faced. So overpowering was Ryan that, in the fifth inning, one of the Detroit players, Norm Cash, marched up to home plate with a paddle instead of a bat. He wasn't allowed to use it, of course; he was simply jesting about how impossible it was to hit Nolan.

14

After seven innings, Ryan had 16 strikeouts. He notched No. 17 in the eighth, and seemed to have a good shot at reaching 20, which would be a record. Then his teammates rallied for five runs, which he was happy to have. But during the long inning, Ryan developed some arm stiffness, which he wasn't happy to have. Nolan went out and retired the Tigers in the ninth. Although he was disappointed that he could not strike out any more batters, he did have something else to feel good about. That night, Nolan Ryan became only the sixth pitcher in baseball history to throw two no-hitters in the same season. "They should change his name to No-Hit Ryan," remarked one writer.

His next outing was against the Baltimore Orioles. Once again, the Ryan Express was blowing batsmen away. The Orioles could not touch him. He held them hitless through five, and again in the sixth and seventh. He was making a strong bid to become only the second man ever to toss back-to-back no-hitters.

Shortstop Mark Belanger led off the eighth. A weak hitter, Belanger was simply trying to make contact. He took a short swing and lofted a short fly beyond the infield. Nobody could reach it. The ball fell for a base hit. "I was lucky to hit it," said Belanger later. "He had unbelievable stuff. The pitch was up and in; he jammed the heck out of me....I just managed to push it over the infield." Ryan had to settle for two no-hitters that season.

Late the following season, 1974, the Angels' film coordinator, George Goodale, had just finished putting together a show about Nolan's two no-hitters. "Now that the film is finished." Goodale told Nolan with a laugh, "don't do anything spectacular tonight."

"Don't worry, I feel terrible," replied Ryan. "But is it all right if I pitch a shutout?" Goodale said that would be fine.

If Nolan felt terrible, the Minnesota Twins must have felt much worse. They not only scored no runs—they did not get any hits. Much to George Goodale's dismay, his film had been made out of date as Nolan smoked his way to his third no-hitter. By the time he picked up No. 4 the next season against the Orioles, a Ryan no-hitter began to seem like a run-of-the-mill occurrence. Only one other pitcher—Sandy Koufax—had fired as many no-hit games.

Not yet 30, Nolan seemed to have plenty of time to secure the record for himself. As his career progressed, he continued to baffle hitters and collect strikeouts at an amazing pace. In fact, he has whiffed more than 3,300 hitters in his career, and is (barring an injury) a cinch to eclipse Walter Johnson's all-time mark of 3,508. He has also thrown seven one-hitters. But the record-breaking fifth no-hitter was eluding him.

A free agent in 1980, Nolan moved back to the National League, joining the Houston Astros. He had only a so-so year in 1980, winning 11 games. But in 1981, he was back to his old, awesome self. Late in the strike-shortened season, he had a 10–4 record and a league-leading 1.74 ERA when he squared off against the Los Angeles Dodgers in a key game in the Western Division pennant race.

Nolan struggled early. He needed 65 pitches just to get through the first three innings. But he seemed to find himself as the innings passed. And as the game moved into the sixth, a sense of excitement began to mount in the Astrodome. The Dodgers had not yet gotten a base hit. He struck out Dusty Baker to end the sixth. The tension in the massive Dome jumped a few notches. Only nine outs separated Ryan from the record.

Dodger catcher Mike Scioscia stepped up in the seventh. Nursing a 2–0 lead, Ryan rocked and fired. Scioscia swung and drove the ball to deep right center. Terry Puhl, the Houston right fielder, was off with the crack of the bat. Streaking to the warning track, he extended his glove and hauled in the long liner. The crowd erupted. Puhl's thievery had kept Nolan Ryan's dream alive. Ryan mowed down the Dodgers without trouble in the eighth. He took the mound for the ninth, now just three outs away.

Leading off with pinch hitter Reggie Smith, a hard-hitting veteran. Nolan pumped three blazers by him for out No. 1. Ken Landreaux moved in. Ryan delivered, and the outfielder tapped a grounder to first —two away. The next batter was the dangerous Dusty Baker. Nolan peered in for the sign from catcher Alan Ashby. Swinging into his motion, he kicked and threw. Baker swung. The ball bounced toward third. Art Howe scooped it up and fired to first. Out! That was it! Nolan Ryan had become the first man ever to toss five no-hitters. The Astros poured out of the dugout to mob their heroic hurler, whom they carried off the field on their shoulders.

The strikeout king at work.

"He said after the third inning that his delivery was messed up, his back was killing him and that he just didn't feel right," said Dave Smith, another Astro pitcher. "Well, mess up my delivery, kill my back, and tell me not to feel right."

"It's hard to believe I got the no-hitter," said Nolan later. "It's the one thing I wanted. I've had a shot at it for a long time. At my age, I thought I wouldn't get it.

"This is by far the most important of my no-hitters," he went on. "I went into the game feeling like I had to do a good job and this turned into one of the biggest games of the year. My others were with ball clubs that weren't doing well and I was still young and trying to get established. When it's all over, this will probably be the one I favor most, being we're in a pennant race, being on national TV, being at home and having my mother here."

Ruth, Nolan's wife, also was on hand, along with other family members. But Nolan "No-Hit" Ryan was bound to feel some extra pride from establishing the record in front of his mother, always one of his toughest critics. "I think it's wonderful what Nolan has accomplished," she remarked once. "But the thing I'm waiting for is a perfect game."

THE PIRATES SURPRISE THE YANKEES IN THE 1960 WORLD SERIES

Baseball, it is often said, is a game of inches. A few inches to the left or right and a foul ball might be a home run. An inch higher and a caught line drive might go for a double up the gap. A pitch just a shade out of the strike zone might make the difference btween a walk and a strikeout. Just about every baseball fan can recall a contest decided by some minute distance, whether it's a ball barely clearing a wall or a bang-bang out call at first base.

But in the heart-stopping finale of the 1960 World Series, a different description of baseball was called for. In that case, baseball was a game of pebbles; because that's what may have decided, more than anything else, who went home a winner and who went home a loser.

The classic pitted the Pittsburgh Pirates against the New York Yankees. The last time the Pirates had won a Series was 35 years earlier, in 1925. The last time the Bucs had been in a Series was 1927, when the Yankees, led by a couple of fellows named Babe Ruth and Lou Gehrig, wiped them out in four straight.

The 1960 Yankees were not exactly slouches with the bat, either. They didn't have Ruth and Gehrig, but they did have Mickey Mantle (40 home runs that season), Roger Maris (39 home runs), and Bill "Moose" Skowron (26 homers). As a team, the Bronx Bombers clubbed 193 round-trippers.

The Pirates had a tough road ahead of them. Though a fine hitting team in their own right with men such as Dick Groat, who hit a league-leading .325, Dick Stuart, Roberto Clemente, and a fine young second baseman, Bill Mazeroski, they were up against a power-packed bunch with a wealth of World Series experience. What's more, the Yankees headed into the Series with a 15-game winning streak. They hadn't lost a game in almost three weeks.

As it turned out this was one fall classic in which streaks and momentum meant nothing. It was impossible—right to the last out—to predict what might happen next. A wild, seven-game affair, the Series was one in which one team set records for runs (55), hits (91), extra-base hits (27), and team batting average (.338)—and lost.

The madness began in Game One, when the Bucs promptly put an end to the Yankee winning streak. The 6–4 triumph was the result of some fine pitching by Vernon Law and Pittsburgh's ace reliever, Roy Face, Groat's batting, and Mazeroski's two r.b.i.'s and homer.

The Yankees must not have taken too kindly to losing the opener. They went on a hitting rampage that temporarily turned the Series into a game of running bases. Round and round the Yanks went, and it seemed as though they would never stop. Behind two homers and five r.b.i.'s from center-fielder Mickey Mantle, the Yankees pasted the Pirates 16–3 in Game Two. Then the Yanks scored six runs in the first inning of the third game (four on a grand slam by second baseman Bobby Richard-son), and never looked back, waltzing to a 10–0 laugher. In two games, the Bucs had been outscored 26–3. They weren't on the run; they were on the gallop.

At least that's the way it seemed before Law came back to hurl Game Four. A 20-game winner during the regular season, he again combined with Face to quiet the New York bats as the Pirates squeaked out a 3–2 decision to even the Series at two games apiece. The next two contests followed a similar pattern: the Pirates won a fairly close one—5–2—in Game Five, and the Yankees, their backs to the wall, won by a rout—12–0—in Game Six. The championship of baseball had come down to one game. Pittsburgh manager Danny Murtaugh elected to cast his fate with Law, who already had come through twice, while New York manager Casey Stengel tabbed Bob Turley, a hard-throwing right-hander who had notched the victory in Game Two.

The 36,683 fans at Pittsburgh's Forbes Field barely had settled into their seats when the fireworks commenced. After a two-out walk to Bob Skinner in the bottom of the first, Rocky Nelson, the Pittsburgh first baseman, hammered a Turley pitch into the right-field stands. A walk and three singles produced

22

two more runs for the Bucs in the second. With Law on the mound, the 4–0 lead looked awfully good. Even after Skowron cracked a homer leading off the fifth, there was no cause for alarm. Law had yielded only three hits and besides, the Bucs had a well-rested Roy Face waiting in the pen.

But the Yanks began to stir things up in the sixth. After Richardson singled and shortstop Tony Kubek walked to lead off the inning, Murtaugh summoned Face, who already had picked up three saves in the Series. The fork baller disposed of Maris on a foul pop, and up stepped Mantle, who singled through the middle to narrow the deficit to 4–2. Two men were on with Yogi Berra at the plate. Face kicked and offered. Berra swung and blasted it into the second deck in right field. A hush fell over the park as Yogi circled the bases. Comfortably ahead just moments ago, the Pirates now trailed 5–4.

With two out in the eighth, the Yankees struck again. A walk, a single, and r.b.i. tallies by Johnny Blanchard and Clete Boyer lifted the Yankee edge to 7–4. The Pirates had only six outs to catch up.

Following a lead-off single by pinch hitter Gino Cimoli, Bill Virdon dug in. Bobby Shantz, a little lefty who had already hurled four innings of shutout relief, peered in for his sign and delivered. Virdon swung, nailing a hard grounder right at shortstop Tony Kubek. It was a perfect double-play ball. Kubek crouched slightly, preparing to field it, when the ball struck a pebble. It took a wild bounce, hopping far over the defenseless shortstop's glove and smacking him squarely in the neck. Kubek fell as though he'd been shot. He had to be replaced by Joe DeMaestri. The

Tony Kubek writhes in pain after being struck in the throat by a grounder. At right, teammate Bobby Richardson calls for help.

Pirate faithful was hoping the bad-hop hit was just the piece of good fortune their team needed. Instead of two out and nobody on, the Bucs had none out and two on.

A single by Groat chased Shantz and cut the New York lead to two. Jim Coates, the new Yankee hurler, picked up two outs on a sacrifice bunt and a fly out, and quickly the Bucs' rally was in serious jeopardy. Next up was Roberto Clemente, who dribbled a slow roller wide of first. Running hard, the fleet outfielder outraced Coates, who was late covering, to the bag. Another run came home on the play. The Pirates had life.

Coates's next challenge was Hal Smith, the Pirates' back-up catcher who had entered the game after starting receiver Smokey Burgess was lifted for a pinch runner. The runners moved off their bases. Coates toed the rubber and delivered. Swinging hard, Smith clouted the ball to deep left. Berra retreated, but it never came down. It was a home run! The three-run blast moved the Bucs back in front, 9–7, with just one inning to play.

The Yanks may have been discouraged, but they didn't hang their heads for long. Richardson and pinch hitter Dale Long stroked singles leading off the ninth, and that was all for Bob Friend, who had relieved Face. Harvey Haddix, the new pitcher, retired the dangerous Roger Maris, but then Mantle laced a single to right center, scoring Richardson and putting runners on the corners with only one out. Tension mounted by the moment as Yogi Berra dug in. Just one run separated the two clubs. Could Haddix hold the slim lead?

He wound and fired, and Berra, always tough in the clutch, smashed a one-hopper to first. Rocky Nelson speared it nicely. But instead of going to second to begin the double play, Nelson stepped on first to retire Berra. Then, whirling around to peg to second, he allowed Mantle to sneak back into first (the force had been removed when Nelson touched first) and, much worse, pinch runner Gil McDougald to scamper home from third. Haddix got the final out, but the damage had been done. The score was 9–9.

Ralph Terry, a right-hander who had come on to get the last out in the eighth, took the hill for the ninth. Bill Mazeroski stepped in, looking to get on base any way he could.

Terry's first pitch was wide of the strike zone. He swung into his wind-up and fired again. The ball came in high and hard. Mazeroski liked the looks of it. He swung. *Crack!* The ball exploded past the infield toward deep left center. Again, Berra raced back. It was gone! A home run! The Pittsburgh Pirates were world champions! Arms waving overhead, the young second baseman bounded around the bases to the plate, where a mob of teammates, fans, and what seemed like half of Pittsburgh swallowed him up.

"I hit a fast ball," said Mazeroski later amid the shouts of joy and sprays of champagne in the Pirate clubhouse. "It was the second pitch, and I knew it was going all the way as soon as it left my bat."

Almost instantly, the Steel City, as the Associated Press reported, "flipped its lid." Traffic came

The welcoming committee greets hero Bill Mazeroski.

to a standstill. Horns honked. Confetti seemed to stream from every window. People literally danced in the streets, and taverns from one end of town to the other overflowed with World Series revelers.

The Yankees had dominated just about every statistical category possible, outscoring, outhitting, and outpitching their opponents. But thanks to Bill Mazeroski, the Pirates were on top in the most important statistic of all: four games to three. To the delirious Pirate fans, after 35 years of waiting, that was all that mattered.

"THE SHOT HEARD
'ROUND THE WORLD"

It was July, 1951, and all was well with the Brooklyn Dodgers. Loaded with potent hitters such as Gil Hodges, Duke Snider, Jackie Robinson, and Roy Campanella, the team was perched atop the National League standings, far above their struggling cross-town rivals, the New York Giants. Brooklyn manager Charlie Dressen liked the way the season was unfolding. When a reporter asked him if he were at all concerned about the Giants, Dressen replied, "The Giants is dead."

Dressen, it turned out, was no better at forecasting than he was at grammar. On August 12, the Giants were 13½ games behind the Dodgers, and Dressen's prediction seemed safer than ever. But from that day forward, the Giants were hotter than the steamy city streets surrounding their ballpark—the Polo Grounds—in upper Manhattan. Paced by sluggers Monte Irvin and Bobby Thomson and a brilliant rookie center fielder named Willie Mays, the Giants mounted a charge for the pennant that has become known as the "Miracle Run."

And it *was* nearly a miracle. At one stretch reeling off 16 straight victories, the Giants won 37 of their last 44 games—an astounding 84 per cent. On the final day of the season, pitcher Larry Jansen, who won 23 games that year, pitched the Giants past the sensational Warren Spahn and the Milwaukee Braves—and into a first-place tie with the Dodgers. The pennant would be decided by a best-of-three play-off.

New York instantly became a city divided by the passions of its baseball fans. The rivalry between the two clubs reached a fever pitch. It seemed the entire city was riveted to radios or televisions as the fierce foes squared off for the pennant.

The Giants took round one. Powered by home runs by Thomson and Irvin, they captured a 3–1 decision in the Dodgers' own park, Ebbets Field. But Brooklyn returned the favor in Game Two, walloping their rivals in the Polo Grounds by a count of 10–0. That meant that one game would decide who would move into the World Series against the New York Yankees. Each team was casting its fate with its top pitcher: Sal Maglie for the Giants, Don Newcombe for the Dodgers.

Brooklyn nicked Maglie for a run in the top of the first on an r.b.i. single by Jackie Robinson. Newcombe, a strapping, 6-foot-4 power pitcher, seemed intent on holding up the slim lead. "He was blinding us," said Monte Irvin.

Irvin saw enough of a Newcombe delivery to double in the seventh inning. He moved to third on a bunt single, and as Bobby Thomson came to the plate, the huge park was gripped with tension. Time for the Giants was running short. Newk delivered, and Thomson lofted a fly ball to deep center. The sacrifice fly enabled Irvin to dash home. The game was tied.

But almost before the Giant fans were finished breathing a sigh of relief, the hated Brooklynites exploded for three runs in the eighth. Newcombe struck out the side in the Giants' half of the inning. Things did not look good for the home team. Down three with only three outs to play, the New Yorkers' long-running miracle seemed destined to expire. Giants' manager Leo Durocher talked to his club before they went to bat. ''You've had some kind of year. You've got nothing to be ashamed of, boys. When you walk off this field, I want your heads right up.''

They weren't ready to walk off just yet. Alvin Dark opened the inning with a single. Don Mueller followed with another. Newcombe settled down to get Irvin on a pop foul, but then Whitey Lockman lashed a double down the left-field line, scoring Dark and leaving runners at second and third. The home-town rooters were going wild. Electricity surged through every nook and cranny of the Polo Grounds. The score was 4–2. A single could tie the game.

Dodger manager Charlie Dressen had seen enough. He lifted Newcombe. Carl Erskine and Ralph Branca were warming in the pen. Branca got the call. Bobby Thomson, the hero of Game One and one of the goats of Game Two—he made two errors at third base in addition to committing a base-running

Bobby Thomson chooses his weapon.

blunder—was the scheduled batter. Rookie Willie Mays was on deck. "I didn't know if they would pitch to Thomson or not," said Durocher afterward. But a widely accepted baseball axiom is that you don't put the go-ahead run on base. Thomson was the go-ahead run. Dressen made no move to pass him.

The National League season had come down to this: two on, one out, bottom of the ninth, the Dodgers leading by two. If Branca could get two men out, the Dodgers would have the pennant. Thomson stepped in, taking the first pitch—strike one. Eyes fixed intently on the big right-hander, Bobby set himself once more. Branca kicked and fired, a high fast ball over the inside part of the plate. Thomson swung. *Crack!* He hit it squarely, rocketing the ball on a low line toward the left-field seats. "Sink, sink," Branca recalled saying as the ball neared the wall. The ball did not obey. It sailed over a helpless Andy Pafko, the Dodger left fielder, into the seats. Thomson had done it! His heroic three-run clout had brought the National League flag to the Polo Grounds. "The Giants win the pennant! The Giants win the pennant!" screamed Russ Hodges, the club's long-time radio announcer. Eight times Hodges repeated those joyous words, as if it had to be said that many times for anyone to believe it.

Instant pandemonium broke loose in the Polo Grounds, almost shaking from all the tumult. Giants players sprinted from the dugout as Thomson joyously circled the bases. The Dodgers stood trancelike, seeming too stunned to move. "I thought all the time there was a chance I could get it," said Pafko later.

"The shot heard 'round the world."

"When the ball went into the stands," said Thomson, "I was more excited than I ever was in my life. A mob of fans poured onto the field. People were trying to rip pieces off my uniform. I thought I could get killed out there. The fans were out of their minds. I took off for the clubhouse weaving through all those people who were trying to get a piece of me."

It was hours before the delirious Giant fans could be coaxed out of the ballpark. The celebration following "The Shot Heard 'Round the World," as the home run has become known, seemed as though it would never end.

In the clubhouse, meanwhile, the disheartened Dodgers dressed silently. The atmosphere, said one reporter, "was like a morgue." Nobody mourned more than Ralph Branca, who threw the pitch and lived in infamy for years afterward. "Oh God, why me, why was I the one?" asked Branca solemnly to no one in particular. The big man cried on the clubhouse steps, his head buried in his arms.

The Dodgers' faithful did not take it much better. Sid Frigand, a newspaper columnist, was on the subway to Brooklyn when the blow was struck. "When I got out at Flatbush and Nostrand Avenues" he remembered, "it was like an atomic bomb had hit. Except for the noise of the vehicles, there was no noise, no talking, no movement."

Jimmy Esposito, the head grounds keeper at Ebbets Field, was out with his men, making preparations on the field for the World Series.

"When Thomson hit the home run, everybody's heart just fell out," he said. Indeed, one swing of Bobby Thomson's bat seemed to make the entire borough of Brooklyn go numb. To have such soaring hopes all season, to have withstood the Giants' charge, and to have been just two outs away from the World Series, and then to have lost it all on one pitch, one swing, and a 315-foot fly ball, was the most heart-breaking finish imaginable to the Dodger fans—who were as passionate and loyal as any fans anywhere.

That the Giants eventually lost to the Yankees in the World Series did not take any luster off the most dramatic comeback in baseball history. They had battled back from the supposedly impossible deficit of 13½ games. And then, down three runs with three outs left in their season, they battled back some more. Finally, they won. So what if the Miracle Run ended there? At least Bobby Thomson and the Giants had proven, beyond any doubt, that Charley Dressen had been wrong—dead wrong—when he said, "The Giants is dead."

A MOST MEMORABLE GAME—
THE RED SOX vs. THE REDS

On a cool autumn evening in New England in 1975, the Boston Red Sox and Cincinnati Reds squared off in a World Series contest. A full moon hung over Boston's Fenway Park like a huge, glow-in-the-dark yo-yo dangling from the black sky. For more than four hours that night, the two league champions went after each other, hooking up in what truly was a fall classic.

Fine pitching, clutch hitting, brilliant fielding—the game had all that and more. Even as it was unfolding, the 35,205 fans who had squeezed into Fenway sensed they were watching one of the most memorable games ever played. The players sensed it, too. Pete Rose, the Reds' stellar third baseman, stepped to the plate with the battle better than three-and-a-half hours old and still deadlocked. He turned to Carlton Fisk, the Boston catcher, and said, "Some kind of game, isn't it?"

Indeed, it was. So much so, in fact, that many baseball people believe the game was largely responsible for lifting baseball out of the doldrums in which it floundered through the early 1970s.

Attendance has increased almost 50 per cent since then, and all signs indicate the following of our national pastime has never been stronger. "The 1975 World Series caught the nation's fancy," noted one major-league official a few years back, "and we're still spinning off from that."

For a time, it looked as though this historic contest would not be played. A steady downpour postponed it for three days before the storm blew out to sea. Finally, Game Six was set to begin.

The Reds were leading the Series, three games to two, and if there was any surprise among baseball fans, it was that the Sox were being so pesky. It was not because the Red Sox did not have a good team. With such stars as Carl Yastrzemski, Carlton Fisk (who rebounded from an injury to bat .331 that season), and sensational rookie center fielder Fred Lynn (who powered home 105 r.b.i.'s to go with his .331 average), the Sox led both leagues in batting with a .275 club average. What's more, they had ended the three-year championship reign of the Oakland A's by besting them in the divisional play-offs.

It's just that the Big Red Machine, as the Cincinnati club had come to be known, was an awesome collection of baseball parts. How else can you describe a team with four men who had won— or would win—Most Valuable Player honors in the National League? Rose had won it. Johnny Bench, widely acclaimed as the best receiver in baseball, had won it twice. Joe Morgan, the pint-sized (5-foot-7) but power-hitting second baseman, captured the prize in '75 and in '76. The slugging left fielder, George Foster, would be so honored in 1977. Toss in stars such as Tony Perez, Dave Concepcion, and Ken Griffey, add one of the game's best bullpens, and it's easy to see why the Reds steamrolled to the Western Division title by an incredible 20 games.

Needing a victory to move the Series into a seventh game, the Sox came out with their bats smoking. Swinging against Cincinnati hurler Gary Nolan, Yastrzemski and Fisk singled in the bottom of the first. That brought up Fred Lynn. Nolan's delivery was greeted with a resounding crack. Lynn's drive carried deep into the right-center-field bleachers. The Fenway faithful went wild. Their beloved Sox had bolted to a three-run lead. With the pitching being handled by Luis Tiant, who had already defeated the Reds twice in the Series with his baffling assortment of deliveries and off-speed pitches, the Sox seemed to be in an enviable position.

Tiant blanked the Reds through the first four frames, yielding only two singles. But in the fifth, the chunky Cuban encountered some trouble. With one out, pinch hitter Ed Armbrister walked and Rose lashed a single up the middle. Up stepped Griffey, who laid into a Tiant offering and belted it deep to left-center. Taking off in pursuit, Lynn raced toward the wall and leaped as high as he could. But the ball was out of reach, and as Lynn slumped to the ground, badly shaken by his collision with the wall, two runs crossed the plate and Griffey steamed into third. Freddie bravely shook off the hurt and stayed in the game, but before the inning was out, Bench had knotted the score at three with a single to left.

The Machine was beginning to roll. Tiant escaped in the sixth, stranding two runners on base. He wasn't so fortunate in the seventh. Griffey and Morgan pounded singles, and with two out, George Foster took his turn. The muscular outfielder smacked Looie's offering off the center-field wall, driving in two runs to lift the Reds to a 5–3 advantage. Tiant got the third out, but there was no joy in Boston; if the Sox couldn't muster a rally, the season would be over in nine outs.

Pedro Bordon, Cincinnati's fifth pitcher of the game (Sparky Anderson, the Reds' manager, was so fond of pulling his pitchers that he had earned the nickname Captain Hook), set the Sox down in order in the seventh. The gloom over New England got worse moments later, when Cesar Geronimo, the weakest hitter in the Cincinnati line-up, drove a ball into the right-field seats for a home run. Darrell Johnson, the Boston manager, relieved Tiant with left-hander Roger Moret, who retired the Reds with no further damage.

The Red Sox had six outs remaining. They were trailing by three. They desperately needed to get something going in the home eighth. Leading off, Lynn stroked a shot up the middle that caromed off Borbon's leg for a single. Rico Petrocelli, the third baseman, worked out a walk. The home-town rooters, with little to cheer about for innings, suddenly sprang to life. The chilly night air was cut by tension. Anderson again went to his pen, calling on one of his aces, Rawly Eastwick. A 24-year-old rookie, Eastwick responded to the pressure like an old pro, picking up two quick outs. Next up was Bernie Carbo, a pinch hitter who had homered once in that role in a previous game.

Eastwick pumped in two quick strikes, then brought a sharp slider to the inside part of the plate. Carbo barely fouled it off. Eastwick swung into his motion and fired again. *Crack!* The ball rocketed high and far toward center. Geronimo darted to the furthest reaches of the park. But it was no use. The ball cleared the fence! Carbo's game-tying clout brought every fan to his feet and every set of lungs to full volume. The noise was deafening. The season was alive.

After Dick Drago came on to put down the Reds in order in the ninth, the Bosox braced for their last licks. Second baseman Denny Doyle got things going with a walk, and Yastrzemski promptly pushed him around to third with a hard single to right. The winning run was only 90 feet away with nobody out. Will McEnaney, Cincinnati's left-handed stopper in the pen, came on and intentionally passed Fisk, setting up a force play at the plate. Fred Lynn stepped in, sacks loaded, still none out.

The center fielder lofted a foul ball down the left-field line, not very deep. Foster caught up to it; Doyle, tagging up on the play, broke for the plate. Foster's peg to Bench nailed him easily. Suddenly, there were two out. Moments later, Petrocelli bounced to Rose to extinguish the Boston threat.

A masterly job by McEnaney had given the Reds a new life. The game went into extra innings.

Following a scoreless tenth, Rose led off the 11th by getting hit by a pitch. With one out, Morgan moved in. He got hold of a Drago pitch and launched it to deep right field. "I haven't got a chance," is how Dwight Evans later described his thought when the ball left Morgan's bat. But he went after it anyway, sprinting all out toward the wall, his back to the infield. Nearing the wall, the graceful right fielder sprang into the air, stretched his body and arm to their fullest, and hauled in the drive by the top of the fence. Instantly, he pivoted and uncorked a strike to first base to double up Griffey, who was approaching third when Evans snagged the ball. Had Evans not caught it, the drive probably would have sailed over the fence. At the very least, Griffey would have scored the go-ahead run.

"If he makes catches like that all the time, I don't ever want to hit one to right," said Pete Rose afterward. "It was like he had magnets in his glove." Sparky Anderson labeled it "the greatest catch I've ever seen." This time, it was the Red Sox who narrowly escaped disaster. Game Six, with more ebbs and flows than an ocean tide, moved into the 12th inning.

Rick Wise, who replaced Drago, flirted with danger when he gave up one-out singles to Perez and Foster. But the right-handed veteran, winner of 19 games that season, came back impressively. He induced Concepcion to pop out and whiffed Geronimo.

Fisk connects...

...And pleads with the ball to stay fair.

Due up for the Sox were Fisk, Lynn, and Petrocelli. On the mound was Pat Darcy, the eighth Cincinnati hurler of the night, tying a Series record. In two innings of work, he had not yielded a hit.

Fisk dug in. Darcy rocked into motion and delivered, a breaking pitch over the plate. *Thwack!* Carlton connected, launching a mile-high fly deep to left. With Fenway Park's short left field, the ball certainly was far enough. The only question was whether it would be fair. Breaking up the first-base line, Fisk fixed his eyes on its orbit and gave it all the help he could. He twisted and turned his body and waved his arms toward fair territory, as if pleading with the vanishing ball to stay fair. And finally, Carlton Fisk leaped into the air and clapped his hands triumphantly; the ball descended into the netting, just inches on the fair side of the foul pole. Instant frenzy broke out in Fenway. Players and fans poured onto the field to greet Fisk at the plate, while the Reds, stunned by the sudden end of the dramatic struggle, filed silently into their clubhouse.

At 12:34 in the morning, four hours and one minute after Luis Tiant fired his first pitch to Fisk, Game Six had come to a fittingly dramatic conclusion.

The spirit of the Big Red Machine took a marked turn for the better less than 24 hours later, when the National League champs squeezed out a 4–3 victory to win the Series. Still, when most fans look back on the 1975 World Series, the first thing they recall isn't that the Reds won, but that the two

45

teams met in one of the most memorable baseball games ever played.

In the words of Pete Rose, a veteran of many baseball battles, Game Six was "the greatest I've ever played in, absolutely the greatest. I'm just proud to be part of the game."

TOM SEAVER
STRIKES OUT 10 IN A ROW

New York Mets fans had come to expect a lot from Tom Seaver. He was touted as "the franchise" almost from the first time he toed the rubber as a rookie in 1967. He was a symbol of hope for the Mets, who had spent five dismal seasons as the lovable losers of the National League. Intelligent, personable, and boyishly handsome, he also was the finest young pitcher in the game. They called him Tom Terrific, and he was.

He launched his career by capturing National League rookie-of-the-year honors in 1967, winning 16 games for a poor team and posting an impressive earned-run average of 2.76. He won 16 more games the following year, lowering his ERA to 2.20. Blessed with a blazing fast ball and pinpoint control—a rare combination—he quickly earned the respect of National League batsmen. "I remember one game when he struck me out with three straight fast balls," recalled Henry Aaron, Tom's boyhood idol. "I just looked out at the kid. He was so cool. I knew then that he was going to be trouble for a long time."

George Thomas Seaver *was* trouble—big trouble

—in 1969, only his third year in the big leagues. Winning 25 games while losing only seven, he had a 2.21 ERA, struck out 208 men and was named the Cy Young Award winner as top pitcher in the National League. More importantly, Seaver capped his brilliant campaign by winning a divisional play-off game and a World Series game, sparking the Miracle Mets to their first world championship. Not long after he was honored as *Sports Illustrated's* Sportsman of the Year.

A lot was expected of him, and Tom Terrific always seemed to deliver. But nobody could have expected even Tom Seaver to accomplish what he did on April 22, 1970. Taking the Shea Stadium hill against the San Diego Padres, Seaver showed from the start that this was a day on which he had all his best pitches working.

Al Ferrara, an outfielder, reached Seaver for a home run in the second inning; outside of that, the fireballing right-hander appeared in complete control. He breezed through the San Diego line-up, allowing only one other hit. Gradually the 14,197 fans began to realize that Seaver, who was blossoming into one of the top strikeout artists in baseball, was whiffing Padres at a remarkable pace. It was not a major-league record pace, but it was not far from one, either.

In the sixth inning, with the Mets clinging to a 2–1 advantage, Ferrara stepped in. Seaver caught him looking at a third strike to retire the side. It was Tom's tenth strikeout of the afternoon. What happened the rest of the way, in the words of one reporter, was "like watching an artist create a masterpiece on canvas."

"The Franchise" fires.

Nate Colbert, a dangerous power hitter, led off the San Diego seventh. Seaver buzzed one past him for out No. 1. Dave Campbell and Jerry Morales followed, and Seaver sent both of them back to the dugout on called third strikes. The Mets' ace had now struck out four in a row and 13 in the game. The record for most strikeouts in a game was 19. The crowd knew Tom would have to strike out every batter for the remainder of the game to equal that mark, and that was almost impossible. But the fans were charged up, anyway; they wanted to see how long Seaver could keep his streak going.

The Mets failed to score, and Seaver took the mound for the eighth. The first batter was Bob Barton. Seaver slipped a third strike past him for five in a row. There weren't many fans on hand for the early-season contest, but they were making enough noise for 50,000. Next up was Ramon Webster, a pinch hitter. Picking up two quick strikes, Tom fired again—swing and a miss. Seaver had six in a row. It also was Seaver's 15th strikeout of the game, tying the club record set by Nolan Ryan. The news flashed on the scoreboard and the fans went berserk. "I wasn't really aware I had that many strikeouts," said Seaver afterward. "I thought I had ten or eleven."

Ivan Murrell, another pinch hitter, stepped in. Three strikes later, he was on his way back to the dugout. A tremendous ovation went up from the crowd as Tom walked off the mound. Not only had he set a new club mark, he also had moved within one strikeout of the major-league record for most consecutive strikeouts. Four pitchers—Johnny Podres, Max

Surfont, Jim Maloney, and Don Wilson—each had whiffed eight hitters in succession. Tension mounted by the second. For once, the fans were rooting for the Met batters to be retired, so anxious were they to see Seaver continue his pursuit of the record.

Making his warm-up tosses before the ninth inning, Seaver knew his task was only going to get harder. The Padres would be bearing down, doing their utmost to at least make contact with the ball. He would have to summon all the strength he could to keep his amazing streak alive.

Van Kelly opened the final frame. Rocking smoothly into his wind-up with each flawless delivery, Seaver blew him away on three pitches, tying the mark of eight strikeouts in a row. Clarence Gaston was the next challenge, the man who stood between Tom Seaver and the record books. The Mets maestro pumped two quick strikes past him. There was only one more to go. Tom gazed in to catcher Jerry Grote, picked up the sign, and reared back and delivered. Gaston did not budge. Umpire Harry Wendelstedt shot up his right arm—strike three! The fans erupted, paying tribute to Tom Seaver, new owner of the major-league record.

One out remained and Seaver, still nursing a one-run lead, knew he could not afford to be careless. The next batter was Al Ferrara, the man who had homered earlier. A final strikeout here would tie Seaver with Steve Carlton for the all-time record of 19 strikeouts in a game.

Ferrara dug in. Seaver rocked and fired—a slider on the outside part of the plate. "Strike one," called

Wendelstedt. Seaver went with the slider again, this time missing. The count was even. Seaver took the rubber once more and unleashed a fast ball. Ferrara swung and missed. Tom Terrific was one strike away, not only from the record, but from concluding the most awesome display of power pitching in baseball history. "I may never come this close again," Seaver remembered telling himself at the time. "I might as well go for it."

Seaver looked in and got his sign. His heart thumping wildly and the fans screaming relentlessly, he broke into his wind-up, putting everything he had into a low, smoking fast ball. Al Ferrara uncoiled from his stance, swinging fiercely. He did not hit it. The ball exploded into Grote's glove. Tom Seaver had done it! He had tied one big-league milestone and established another by whiffing an unbelievable 10 men in a row. No Padre had hit the ball since the sixth inning.

"I might have thrown a different pitch in a situation like this," remarked Seaver later, discussing the final pitch. "The pitch probably should have been a slider outside. ...I was thinking about Ferrara as far back as the eighth inning. I remember he had hit a home run off my fast ball earlier. I was still worried about him, but I had to challenge him. So I just let the fast ball rip. I was that close, and I wanted it."

Johnny Podres, whose record Seaver had broken, happened to be on hand that day. "He was fantastic, outstanding," said the former Dodger great. "There was no doubt in my mind he would break the record. He had perfect rhythm. As hard as he was throwing, he was still hitting the spots. If you didn't swing, it was a strike."

Seaver whiffs Ferrara for No. 10 in a row.

Catcher Jerry Grote was equally enthusiastic. "He was like a machine those last few innings. ...He had perfect stuff. He was just blowing the ball in there. The batters couldn't touch him. I don't see how any pitcher could have been better." No doubt the San Diego Padres would have agreed.

"Another night, another game," said Seaver jokingly to a swarm of media people who engulfed him after his record-shattering effort. But later he spoke more seriously about what his performance meant. "I did feel a sense of accomplishment, of further having proved myself." He continued proving himself the rest of the year, piling up 283 strikeouts to lead the league. It was only the third of the nine consecutive seasons in which he struck out 200 or more hitters, a major-league record. He also set the mark for most seasons with 200 or more strikeouts in a career (10).

"I can shut everything else from my mind when I am bearing down on any one thing," Tom observed once, touching on one of the keys to his success. "And that enables me to do it better. All you owe the world and yourself is to make the best use of your talents. I am dedicated to this. Dedication and concentration are the deciding factors between who wins and who loses."

A three-time Cy Young Award winner, Tom Seaver has won more than 250 games over his career. He has pitched five one-hitters—tying another National League mark—and a no-hit game, and sent more than 3,000 batters down on strikes since he first arrived on the major-league scene. Ten of those went down in succession, and of all his marvelous accomplishments, that may be Tom Seaver's most memorable.

GRAIG NETTLES'S GOLDEN
GLOVE SAVES THE DAY

Two fans were slowly making their way through the huge Yankee Stadium crowd minutes after the end of Game Three of the 1978 World Series. "The Yanks were lucky to win it," said one. "They got by by the skin of their teeth."

The Yankees, to be perfectly accurate, did no such thing. What they did was escape by the webbing of Graig Nettles's glove. Nettles played third base, a position where the ball is often hit so hard and arrives so fast that it is known in baseball jargon as the "hot corner." On a warm Friday afternoon, during an absolutely critical game for the Yankees if they wanted to defend their World Series crown, Graig Nettles handled the hot corner coolly and brilliantly. He may well have given the finest fielding performance by a single player in any World Series game in history.

As far as the Yankees were concerned, Nettles's timing could not have been better. Trailing the Los Angeles Dodgers two games to none, the Yankees were counting on their lithe left-hander, Ron Guidry, to turn the Series around. It seemed a good bet.

For the entire 1978 season, Guidry was as unbeatable as any pitcher has ever been. He won 25 games and lost only three, and the dazzling combination of his fast ball and slider often made opposing hitters look as though they were using toothpicks instead of bats. But against the Dodgers, the Louisiana native wasn't sharp. He yielded eight hits, walked a season-high seven batters, and constantly was surrounded by Dodger base runners. Yet he maintained his winning ways, gaining credit for a 5–1 Yankee triumph. There's no way he would have were it not for the golden glove of Mr. Nettles.

The power-hitting third baseman had been the anchor of the New York infield since coming by trade from the Cleveland Indians in 1972. Originally, he signed with the Minnesota Twins as a second baseman. "After my first year," Nettles recalled, "they asked me to move to third base, and I wanted to know why. They told me that they had another guy who was one class ahead of me who looked like he was going to be pretty good at second base. His name was Carew." That was Rod Carew, seven-time American League batting champion. One look at Carew's swing convinced Graig to reconsider his career plans. He made the switch to third base. And he has been robbing batters of hits ever since. Just ask the Dodgers.

The Nettles show began in the third inning. With one on and two out, the Yanks leading 2–1, Reggie Smith lashed a wicked line drive down the third-base line. Nettles reacted instantly, flinging himself to the ground and backhanding the ball deep behind the bag. He quickly jumped to his feet and fired to first to nip Smith and end the uprising. The 56,447 fans roared in appreciation of the clutch glovework. They hadn't seen anything yet.

Smith again was the victim of Nettles's magic in the fifth. Two runners were on and two were out when the switch-hitting slugger pulled another blast over third. Airborne, Nettles made a glittering backhanded stop to hold to a single a ball that looked like a sure double. The play saved at least one run and maybe two.

The next batter was Steve Garvey, the Dodgers' hard-hitting first baseman. Guidry fired, and Garvey rocked a ground smash down the line. Craig hit the dirt one more time, diving all out toward the bag. The ball stopped there, as Nettles snared it cleanly and swiftly threw to second for the inning-ending force out. It was his third sparkling play in five innings. A thunderous ovation filled the historic stadium as Graig trotted off the field. So breath-taking was Nettles's display that even Preston Gomez, the Dodger third-base coach, paid him tribute, applauding briefly after one of his sterling stabs. Baseball coaches do not often clap for an opposing player—particularly when that player is single-handedly breaking his team's back.

With Guidry still struggling, the sacks again were loaded with Dodgers in the sixth. Up stepped second baseman Lopes, who cracked a Guidry pitch toward the human vacuum cleaner manning third base. Nettles vaulted to his right, horizontal to the ground, and flagged down the searing liner on a

An airborne Nettles frustrates the Dodgers once again.

hop. He scrambled to his feet and delivered a strike to second for the force. Lopes glared at Nettles, as if to say, "Hey, enough is enough for one game."

One inning later, Thurman Munson singled home one run and Reggie Jackson brought home two. The rally broke the game open. But it wasn't a bat that decided Game Three of the 1978 World Series. It was a glove, and it belonged to Graig Nettles.

"Nettles kept Guidry in the game," said Los Angeles shortstop Bill Russell.

"It was the greatest exhibition I've ever seen," said Lopes, Nettles's fourth victim. Echoing Lopes's sentiments was Los Angeles manager Tom Lasorda, who agreed it was "one of the greatest exhibitions of playing third base I've seen in all my career."

Yankee skipper Bob Lemon was equally awed. "I've seen a lot of great plays in 41 years, and I'd have to compare him to Brooks Robinson." But for many of the Yankee players, watching Nettles make fantastic, flopping grabs was a routine experience.

"So what's new?" asked Reggie Jackson in the clubhouse after the game. "Nettles made the plays. Nettles always makes the plays. I've seen him throw the ball away twice in 350 games I've been here. The man is the best."

"I think what he did," joked Guidry, "was give me back all the ones he missed during the season." Guidry acknowledged that this was one day when he needed all the support he could find. "I had it in the bullpen," he said of his pitching form. "And that's where I left it. ...I just decided not to try to over-throw. I just had to resort to something else."

How did Nettles do it? Don't ask Graig. "The hardest part of the game is trying to explain the plays," he said to the mob of media people who surrounded him after the contest. "They're all instinctive plays. There are no long explanations involved. The ball is hit, and I react to it. I don't know how many runs I've saved, things were happening too fast. I just know I saved some."

The Yankees went on to win three more games and take the Series, four games to two. There were many people who felt Graig Nettles, in spite of his lackluster hitting in the six games (four hits in 25 at-bats for a .160 average), should have won the Most Valuable Player Award. Instead, honors went to shortstop Bucky Dent, who collected 10 hits in 24 trips for a .417 average and seven r.b.i.'s.

But without Nettles's flawless fielding—he handled 18 chances in the series without an error—the Dodgers almost certainly would have chased Guidry in Game Three. And no team has ever won a Series after being down three games to none. As one writer put it, "If Nettles had hit just a little bit, he would have walked off with MVP. Personally, I don't care if he hit .000, he's still the man who turned it around."

Reggie Smith, who was robbed twice by the webbing of Graig Nettles's glove, could not have agreed more. "Not taking anything away from Guidry," he said, "but the Series score is really Dodgers two, Nettles one."

THE MOST HEARTBREAKING
GAME EVER PITCHED

It looked as though the skies might open up any minute. The cold, damp night air hung heavily over Milwaukee's County Stadium. It was late May of 1959 and, all in all, a dreary evening to be outside.

Harvey Haddix, who was battling a heavy cold, probably should have been in bed. And he probably would have been, except that he had a scheduled engagement for that night. A hurler for the Pittsburgh Pirates, Haddix was due to take the mound against the Braves—cold or no cold. So he spent the afternoon in bed, saving what strength he had for his evening's chores.

He wasn't the sort of pitcher who had power to spare. Only 5-foot-9 and 160 pounds, Haddix relied on a deceptively quick fast ball, an assortment of breaking pitches, and sharp control to put down opposing batters. He broke in with the St. Louis Cardinals in 1953, drawing rave reviews by winning 20 games. But the 33-year-old southpaw had never been able to duplicate that success. Bouncing from the Cincinnati Reds to the Philadelphia Phillies before being acquired by the Pirates, he was no more than a journeyman starter. There wasn't a prophet in the land who could have predicted what was to happen that night in Milwaukee.

If he had any shot at all at winning, Haddix knew he had to be sharp. County Stadium had a well-deserved reputation for being a home-run hitter's paradise, and the Braves were a hard-hitting outfit. With sluggers such as Eddie Mathews, Joe Adcock, and Henry Aaron—one of the best young players in the National League—they were not a team to be taken lightly. The New York Yankees found that out the hard way, losing to the Braves in the 1957 World Series and barely beating them the following year. Another factor Harvey had to contend with was his mound opponent, Lew Burdette, one of the top pitchers in the league.

Haddix had to be encouraged by the first two innings, as he set down the first six Braves to face him. In the top of the third, the Pirates tried to get things going against Burdette, a wily veteran who had long been suspected of throwing a spitball now and again. With one on and one out, Haddix stepped up, looking to help his own cause. A good-hitting pitcher, the little lefty smacked a liner up the middle that caromed off Burdette's leg toward second base. Running hard with the swing, Roman Mejias, a Pirate outfielder, rounded second and decided to gamble and try for third. Milwaukee shortstop Johnny Logan ran down the loose ball and pegged to third. Mejias was a dead duck.

There was plenty of room for second-guessing Mejias's base running because the next Pirate batter, shortstop Dick Schofield, singled to right, a hit that easily would have scored a runner from second. A fly out ended the inning. The Pirates had three hits in one inning and had failed to score. Managers hate to see opportunities such as that squandered, particularly against a pitcher of Burdette's caliber.

Haddix sailed through the next three frames, setting down each of the nine men he faced. The only Brave to come close to reaching base was Logan, who lashed a liner to short that Schofield snared with a leaping grab. With one out in the sixth, it was Logan's turn again. Haddix offered, and the infielder shot a ground ball deep into the hole between third and short. Moving quickly to his right, Schofield backhanded the ball, braced himself, and fired a strike to first to nip Logan. Burdette followed with a strikeout, and as the game turned into the seventh, the crowd of 19,194 began to buzz with excitement. It was raining now and the Braves weren't doing a thing, but there was something very special in the works. Harvey Haddix, the fans began to realize, had allowed neither a hit nor a base runner. Eighteen Braves had marched to the plate, and all 18 went right back to the dugout.

Burdette, matching Haddix goose egg for goose egg, squared off against Bob Skinner, a Pittsburgh outfielder, in the seventh. Skinner connected solidly, launching a long fly to right. When the ball left the bat, it seemed certain that the clout would ring up the game's first run. But the swirling wind held it up, and Aaron was able to haul it in at the wall. Haddix, no doubt beginning to wonder what he had to do to get a run, breezed through the seventh and eighth. Their rooting interests aside, the appreciative Braves' fans stood and cheered for Harvey Haddix after each inning. They knew they were witnessing one of the finest pitching performances of the season. What they did not know yet was that it would turn out to be the finest pitching performance of *any* season.

The Pirates threatened once more in the ninth. They collected two hits against Burdette, who would bend but wouldn't break. The right-hander got out of the jam when Skinner lined out to first.

Haddix, who lost a no-hit bid in the ninth inning back in his rookie season, came out for the ninth. Later, Haddix said he knew he had a no-hitter, but didn't realize he had a perfect game; he thought he had walked someone in the early innings. In any case, he knew what he did not have was a victory—not yet, anyway. Every batter was critical. One mistake could mean the game. Bearing down, Haddix whiffed center fielder Andy Pafko, then induced Logan to fly out. Only one batter—Burdette—stood between Haddix and baseball immortality. Only seven men in the previous 80 years had managed to retire every batter they had faced in a nine-inning game. Haddix pitched to his opponent as intently as if he were Babe Ruth. Harvey picked up a couple of strikes, and peered in for the sign. Winding and kicking, he fired again. Burdette swung—and missed! Haddix had retired

27 straight men! Now, if his team could push across just one measly run...

With one out in the 10th, Don Hoak stroked a single. Next up was pinch hitter Dick Stuart, a big strong man who once walloped 66 homers in one minor-league season. Burdette delivered, and Stuart swung, driving a towering fly ball to the furthest reaches of center field. It seemed certain it would carry over the fence, but again the wind played a cruel trick on Haddix and the Bucs. The ball could not fight through the gale, and Pafko snatched it. It was just another out.

On the hill in the 10th, Haddix began to show signs of weariness. Del Rice, a pinch hitter, drove Bill Virdon to deep center before the Pirate out-fielder hauled in his long fly. Eddie Mathews followed with a shot almost to the identical spot, but Virdon was there once more. Aaron grounded out, but the two prior hits were an indication (one of the few all night) that Haddix was, after all, human.

The deadlock seemed unbreakable. The game moved into the 11th, then the 12th; the only thing that was mounting faster than the zeroes was the tension. The crowd, now firmly in Harvey's corner, seemed to wait breathlessly for every pitch, wondering how long the Buc hurler could be perfect. already he'd pitched the longest no-hitter in baseball history and he'd become the first man ever to pitch a perfect game for more than nine innings. Burdette, meanwhile, may not have been perfect. But he was plenty good enough.

Haddix, showing astonishing endurance, seemed

Haddix shows his "perfect" form.

to get a second wind in the 12th, mowing down the Braves with apparent ease—a bouncer to the mound, a medium fly ball, and a grounder. In the top of the 13th, Burdette allowed a two-out single to Schofield—the Pirates' 11th hit of the night—but the Bucs stopped there. Pittsburgh manager Danny Murtaugh asked Harvey if he wanted to come out. Having hurled the greatest game of all time, the manager suggested that Haddix had done his job quite well that night. Haddix said he wanted to keep going.

Leading off the bottom of the 13th was second baseman Felix Mantilla, a late-inning replacement. Haddix, who had splendid control all night—he went to three balls on only one batter—quickly pumped two strikes past the young infielder. He kicked and fired again. Haddix thought he had Mantilla struck out. Plate umpire Vinnie Smith thought otherwise; he called the pitch a ball.

Undaunted, Haddix came back with another fine pitch to Mantilla, who bounced it harmlessly toward third. Don Hoak scooped it up easily, casually glanced at the ball as he took it from his glove and pegged to first. It was a routine play, the sort a major leaguer makes 99 per cent of the time. Unfortunately for Haddix, this was the other one per cent. Hoak threw the ball in the dirt, well in front of the bag, and first baseman Rocky Nelson could not come up with it. After 12 remarkable innings and 36 batters, Harvey Haddix's perfect game was history.

But it was no time to bemoan the misplay. The game was still scoreless, and Haddix still had his no-hitter. After a sacrifice bunt and an intentional walk to Aaron, Joe Adcock, Milwaukee's power-hitting first baseman, stepped in. Adcock took the first pitch for ball one. Haddix wound and delivered once more, a breaking pitch up and over the plate. Adcock tore into it, blasting it deep to right center. Virdon dashed back and leaped at the fence. The slick center fielder gave it his all. But it wasn't enough. The ball cleared the fence. With one fatal blow, the masterpiece that Haddix had been creating for nearly three hours was destroyed. It all went for nought; the no-hitter, the shutout, even the win. They all were wrenched away from Haddix by one swing of Joe Adcock's bat.

The memorable contest had an unusual conclusion. While Adcock circled the bases, Aaron, thinking the ball was in play, ran only to second and (with Mantilla having scored the game-winning run) headed back to the dugout. The result was that Adcock passed Henry on the bases, which calls for an automatic out. Not until the next day were things sorted out; Adcock was given credit only for a double and 1 r.b.i. Thus the final score was 1–0, even though Adcock actually had hit a home run.

Of course, none of this mattered one bit to Harvey Haddix, who some 15 years later said, "It still hurts." And why shouldn't it? Of the thousands and thousands of games that have been pitched over the decades in the big leagues, Harvey Hadix had pitched what was without question the

Harvey snags a comebacker.

best one of all. And he lost. "I thought I had Mantilla struck out on the pitch before," said Harvey, recalling the start of the 13th. "If the umpire had called it a strike, Mantilla would have been out of there. I'll never forget that play. Hoak had all night after picking up the ball. He looked at the seams...then threw it away." Of the ball hit by Adcock, Harvey said it was "my only bad pitch. I tried to keep a slider down and away. But I got it up too high."

And so the best game ever pitched also was the most heartbreaking. As Bill Virdon said in the solemn Pirate clubhouse, "A pitcher does this once in a lifetime—once in baseball history—and we can't win the game for him."

THE YANKEES'
COMEBACK SEASON

Boston Red Sox fans have a well-deserved reputation for being among the most rabid and loyal rooters in baseball. Spread from Connecticut to Maine, they blanket the New England landscape as densely as a February snowstorm, pulling for their beloved Sox through good times and bad. For most of this century, the times have leaned more on the bad side. The last time a world-championship flag was hoisted over Boston's Fenway Park was 1918, when a sensational young left-handed pitcher named Babe Ruth hurled two World Series triumphs. Pennants haven't exactly streamed in, either. Since the Babe's heroics in 1918, the Sox have managed to win just four American League titles.

It's easy to understand, given their club's history, why the long-suffering Red Sox fans were beside themselves with joy for most of the summer of 1978. That edition of the Sox, managed by a round, tobacco-chewing man named Don Zimmer, appeared to be one of the most invincible outfits ever assembled. By mid-July, Boston had racked up 61 victories against only 28 losses. The closest rival, the

Milwaukee Brewers, were eight games back. The Sox had one of their finest pitching staffs in years, headed by Dennis Eckersley, a 20-game winner they had pried away from the Cleveland Indians. But the biggest reason why the Sox were riding high was a line-up loaded with baseball mashers: Fred Lynn, Carl Yastrzemski, Rick Burleson, Dwight Evans, and the main masher, Jim Rice, the muscle-bound outfielder who wound up the season with 46 homers, 139 r.b.i.'s, 213 hits, a .315 average, and 406 total bases—the most by an American Leaguer since the days of Joe DiMaggio.

Cruising along with the best record in the majors, Boston seemed a shoo-in for the Eastern Division title, the pennant and, in all likelihood, the World Series. Even playing only .500 baseball the rest of the way probably would be enough to win the division, unless another club got red hot. By playing so superbly over the first half of the year, Boston had the luxury of not really worrying about the opposition; barring a total collapse, the Sox would be in fine shape.

Certainly, during those high-flying days of midsummer, their last concern was the New York Yankees. True, the Bronx Bombers were their arch-rivals (a feud that has been running between the two cities since the Yanks bought Babe Ruth for $100,000 from the Sox in 1919, a move that launched the Yankees on their way to decades of baseball dominance). And true, the New Yorkers were the reigning champions of baseball and kings of the American League for two years running. But it was equally true that the Yanks were a team on the verge of self-destruction. Ravaged by pitching injuries and wracked by dissension, they were mired in fourth place, 14 games behind the Sox. Manager Billy Martin was about to be fired and replaced by Bob Lemon. Slugger Reggie Jackson was unhappy and so, it seemed, was half the team. Gripes were aired daily in the New York press. The Yankees were a team going nowhere. Their chances of defending their crown seemed nil. At least that's the way it looked some 90 games into the season.

But baseball has a 162-game season, and just when it appeared they were buried, the Yankees began digging themselves out. Sparked by a bunch of tough and talented old pros—Jackson, Thurman Munson, Roy White, Lou Piniella, and Graig Nettles—the Yankees started winning in clusters. A coinciding slide by the Red Sox helped New York climb to within six-and-a-half games by the first of August.

The Sox stiffened, holding the Yankees at bay for the rest of the month. But with September came a swoon for the Sox and a surge for the Yankees. Boston dropped 14 of 17 contests while the Yankees were winning 15 of 16. Included in those streaks was a four-game set in Fenway that has been dubbed the Boston Massacre. New York swept all four, outscoring the Red Sox 42–9. What a turnaround! By the middle of the month, Boston was three-and-a-half games back and fading fast.

Red Sox fans thought they had endured every heartbreak imaginable over the years, but this was the limit. To blow a lead like that was just about unforgivable. Grumbling about the team's ineptitude reached an all-time high. And then, at the season's darkest hour, the Red Sox fashioned a mini-miracle—a stunning comeback of their own. It wasn't as dramatic or impressive as the Yankees' turnaround, but it showed tremendous spirit and determination. And it was enough to tie the Yankees for first on the last day of the season.

The divisional title would be decided by a one-game play-off. A coin was tossed. The Red Sox won. The game would be played in Fenway Park. On the hill for Boston was Mike Torrez, a former Yankee who had been the pitching hero of the team's World Series triumph over the Dodgers the season before. But Torrez was a free agent and, when the Yankees did not make an offer he liked, he elected to sign with the Red Sox. He had plenty of incentive to beat his ex-mates.

For the Yanks, the mound was manned by their extraordinary southpaw, Ron Guidry, who was coming off what many believe was the finest season ever by any pitcher. He had won 24 and lost only three, tossed nine shutouts, had an ERA well under 2.00, and had struck out 18 batters in one game. Nobody has yet figured out how Guidry, a power pitcher, can throw a baseball so hard with his 5-foot-11, 160-pound body. But the Yankees weren't asking questions; they were overjoyed to have him on the mound for this 163rd game.

The stage was set for the conclusion of what was perhaps the craziest pennant or divisional race ever.

Ron Guidry got the call for the Yanks.

Like two fighters coming out for the fifteenth round of a dead-even championship bout, they knew all they had worked for had come down to this. The setting could not have been more perfect; the sky was a rich blue, the air clear and autumn-crisp.

The Sox struck the initial blows. Following a scoreless first, Yastrzemski measured a Guidry pitch and ripped it just inside the right-field foul pole for a home run. Torrez looked determined to make that lone tally stand up, zipping the Yankees one inning after another.

The Yankees were concerned that Guidry, pitching on three days' rest, might not be at his overpowering best; in the sixth inning it appeared that was the case. Burleson began the uprising with a fierce line-drive double to left. A sacrifice bunt later, Jim Rice rang up run No. 2 with a solid single to center. Then, with two out, after Fisk was passed intentionally, Fred Lynn crunched a ball on a low line toward right. Piniella, off with the crack of the lefty's bat, broke toward the line. Nearing the wall, he extended his glove and speared the ball to rob Lynn of a certain double and the Sox of at least two more runs. Still, Lou's catch would not count for much if the Yanks could not get their bats going.

Limited to three hits at that point, New York finally started some trouble with one out in the seventh. Back-to-back singles by Chris Chambliss and Roy White put the tying runs on board. Pinch hitter Jim Spencer flied to left for the second out. Shortstop Bucky Dent stepped in.

On a 1–0 count, the handsome infielder smacked

the ball straight down into his left ankle, a spot he's hit repeatedly over the season. He fell to the ground in pain. Hoping to shake off the sting so he could continue, he hobbled around near the Yankee dugout. On orders from Mickey Rivers, the Yankee center fielder, a batboy handed Bucky a new bat, saying, "Mickey says this is the good one." Dent didn't give it much thought.

He dug back in. Torrez rocked and delivered, a fast ball up and in. Dent went after it, connecting solidly for a high fly to deep left. Yaz raced back, positioning himself to play the ball off the Green Monster, Fenway's 37-foot left-field wall that—being only 315 feet from home plate—looms as every pitcher's enemy. He never got the chance. Dent's shot carried just over the top. It was a home run by a player who had hit only four all year long. Just like that, the Yankees vaulted to a 3–2 lead. "I thought I jammed him enough," said Torrez later. "I was so darned shocked when it went out. I thought it was just a fly ball off the wall. Then, 'Oh my God!'"

A walk and a stolen base later, Torrez was gone and Bob Stanley, a sinker-balling righty, was in. Munson greeted him with a double to left to increase the Yanks' lead to 4–2. When Reggie Jackson led off the eighth with a mammoth homer to center, the Yankees, who had been coming back all year, looked as though they finally had put their New England rivals to rest. What's more, Guidry had been replaced by Rich "Goose" Gossage, a flame thrower who was the top relief pitcher in the

77

league. But then, the Red Sox had also proven themselves to be a pretty fair comeback team. And they showed it again.

Jerry Remy stroked a double leading off the Boston eighth, and with one out Yaz brought him home with a single. Singles by Fisk and Lynn nudged the Sox to within a run—5-4—with the tying run at second, the winning run at first, and only one out. Gossage, for one of the few times all season, was being pummeled. The Boston fans were delirious. The Yankees were on the run, but manager Bob Lemon elected to stay with the Goose, who rewarded the manager's faith by getting the next two outs without further damage.

The Yankees went down quietly in the ninth, and the entire season in the American League East had come down to three outs. They had battled each other all season. They each had won 99 games. They were the best teams in baseball and just happened to be in the same division. Now, with one inning to play in the 163rd game, only one run separated them.

Gossage retired pinch-hitter Dwight Evans on a fly ball for out No. 1, but then Burleson worked the hurler for a walk. Remy stepped in and, with his compact, punchy swing, drove a liner to right. Piniella charged, and then, holding up his hands, lost the ball in the sun. It bounced in front of him for a hit, but he prevented further trouble by snagging the ball on one hop just a split second before it could kick past him. Piniella fired the ball in and Burleson, running cautiously, stayed at second, though it appeared he could have made third easily.

Bucky Dent: The unlikely home-run hitter broke a lot of hearts in Fenway Park.

The play had huge consequences. The next Bosox batsman, Rice, flied deep to right. Had Burleson been on third he would have scored easily on the tag up. Instead he could only advance to third. The Sox had one out left. Their hopes rode on the bat of their venerable superstar, Carl Yastrzemski.

So it was down to this—a classic confrontation between a great pitcher and a great hitter. Goose's first offering was off the mark. Ball one. He peered in for a sign and, arms and legs a whirl of motion, rocked and fired again. Yaz uncoiled and whipped his bat around. The ball lofted high and harmlessly in foul territory near third. Sox fans pleaded silently for it to carry into the seats, but to no avail. Graig Nettles moved under it and closed his glove around it. Gossage leaped into the air and the Yanks streamed from the dugout. The greatest comeback in baseball history was complete.

The Yankees went on to beat the Dodgers in the World Series. But to a lot of fans, even that lofty achievement was an anticlimax after the 163rd game because, on a brilliant fall day in New England, the drama could not have been any greater, nor the baseball any better.

HANK AARON'S
715th HOME RUN

For nearly 30 years, the number 714 had a very special place in baseball's record books. It marked the ultimate achievement—the number of lifetime home runs—of the ultimate ballplayer, Babe Ruth, the man voted the greatest player who ever stepped on a diamond.

So sacred was the feat, so far beyond the abilities of any other man, that people treated the record as though it were etched in stone, never to be challenged, let alone broken. After all, the greatest sluggers in the game's history—Ted Williams, Willie Mays, Mickey Mantle, and company—all had taken aim at the mark, and all had fallen considerably short. All, that is, except one.

As the 1974 baseball season unfolded, the attention of baseball fans the world over was fixed squarely on the muscular shoulders of Henry Louis Aaron of the Atlanta Braves. Hammerin' Hank, as they called him, was on the verge of breaking the unbreakable, looking to go where no home-run hitter had ever before ventured: he was going beyond Babe Ruth.

The glare of the spotlight never dimmed in the latter stages of Aaron's career. As he closed in on the Babe, he was besieged by a horde of reporters everywhere he played. Every ball he knocked over the fence was big news. The questions never stopped, and neither did the pressure. It's not easy chasing a legend; Hank found that out the hard way. Mail poured in and, sadly, some of it was written by bigoted, small-minded people who hurled racist slurs at Aaron and expressed horror that a black man could have the gall to challenge the accomplishments of a white man. Henry Aaron naturally was dismayed by such attitudes, but he handled the situation with the quiet grace and dignity that had become as much of his trademark as his power-packed, right-handed stroke. "All I want is to be treated as a human being," he said once. "What do they want me to do? Stop hitting home runs? I have no intention of making people forget Babe Ruth. I just want to be sure they remember Hank Aaron."

Perhaps more than anyone in baseball history, Hank Aaron was a forgotten superstar. The final, fame-filled seasons of his 24-year career were a stark contrast to most of the earlier ones. He began with the Braves, then playing in Milwaukee, in 1954—a 20-year-old kid from Mobile, Alabama who left home to play pro ball with two dollars in his pocket, a cardboard suitcase in his hand, but with a swing that prompted one scout to call him "one of the finest natural hitters God ever put on this earth."

Aaron first attracted the attention of major-league scouts as a 17-year-old shortstop for the Indiana

Clowns of the Negro League. Pencil-thin at 5-foot-11 and 155 pounds, he had an unusual cross-handed batting style, which a coach finally convinced him to abandon. He wasn't comfortable with the accepted method at first, but you never would have known that to watch him hit. He terrorized the league, hitting well over .400 through most of the season. Dewey Griggs, a scout for the Braves, urged his club to meet the Clowns' $7,500 asking price for the youngster. "The kid's worth $7,500 just for his swing," raved Griggs. "I'd make the down payment out of my own pocket."

Other scouts felt the same way. In fact, a talent hunter for the New York Giants reached a preliminary agreement with the clowns and offered Henry $250 per month to play in their farm system. Griggs quickly countered with a $300-per-month offer. The Giants declined to get into a bidding war, a decision that has left a lot of Giant fans second-guessing over the years; for an extra $50 a month, the Giants might well have had the finest pair of outfielders ever to play together—Willie Mays and Henry Aaron.

Hank played in the minor leagues for two seasons, won a Most Valuable Player Award in each, and reported to spring training in 1954, a 20-year-old trying to latch on to the big club. Not long after, Braves' right fielder Bobby Thomson suffered a break and Hank Aaron got one. The veteran, side-lined by a fractured ankle, was replaced by the rookie. Aaron made an immediate impression. "The first time I saw him hit a home run," said center fielder Billy Bruton, "the shortstop leaped for the ball, thinking he could catch it."

"Magic is the only way to describe it," added Thomson of Aaron's swing. "You had this feeling even then that this guy was something special."

Thomson and the Braves may have known that, but it took most of the rest of the world a good long while to catch on. "Henry Aaron," in the words of writer James Toback, "like sunsets, music, and summer, is taken for granted." Part of it was that Henry broke in on a team with established stars such as Eddie Mathews, the slugging third baseman, and pitchers Warren Spahn and Lew Burdette. Nor did it help Henry to have come up about the same time as two fellows named Mays and Mantle, both immense talents and both playing in New York (the Giants did not move to San Francisco until 1958).

You simply can't get the kind of attention or recognition outside New York that you can get in it," said Henry. "There's something about the fans there, their intensity, their enthusiasm, even their rage, that lights up a special kind of fuse that might be a prerequisite for real stardom in any sport."

There also was, as Henry acknowledged, "the matter of style. It's just not my way to be flashy or flamboyant the way, say, Willie is. I have my own even rhythm, and I guess it just doesn't attract the kind of attention that a more colorful style does." The Aaron style, rather, was one of grace and efficiency. He never seemed to waste any motion or energy. When he would come up to bat, he always would walk very slowly toward the plate, almost as if he had just been awakened.

A superb outfielder, too, Aaron leaps for
a long drive.

"My daddy always told me, 'Henry, never hurry unless you have to,'" said Aaron. How quickly he came to life with a bat in his hands. The strength of his wrists and forearms was legendary.

"Trying to sneak a fast ball by Henry Aaron," remarked Curt Simmons, a pitcher who faced him many times, "is like trying to sneak the sun past a rooster." Added Warren Spahn, the Braves' Hall-of-Fame hurler: "It's fantastic how long Henry can look at a pitch. It's like giving him an extra strike."

Others may have been commanding the headlines, but young Henry Aaron wasted little time commanding the respect of the pitchers in the National League. He belted 27 home runs in his second year, led the league in hitting with a .328 mark in his third, and in his fourth—1957—he walloped 44 homers and drove in 132 runs and was honored as the league's Most Valuable Player. He capped off the campaign by hitting .393 with three homers and seven r.b.i.'s in the World Series, sparking the Braves past the powerful New York Yankees. He also became a participant in one of baseball's most famous conversations. As Henry came up to bat, Yankee catcher Yogi Berra noticed the 23-year-old slugger was holding the bat in an odd way. "Hey kid, you're holding the bat wrong," said Yogi. "You're supposed to have the trademark up."

"I didn't come up here to read," replied Henry. "I came up here to hit."

And hit he did. Season after season, Hank kept on hammering homers. He passed the 200 mark in 1960, 400 in 1966, and 600 in 1971. He cracked an amazing 40 home runs at age 39 to become the only man other than the Babe to break the 700 barrier. Number 700 came off Ken Brett of the Philadelphia Phillies. The crowd at Atlanta Stadium went berserk, twice demanding Aaron emerge from the dugout for a "curtain call." "I didn't think it would be this much," said Henry with characteristic modesty. "I thought it was just another homer." Aaron went on to clout 13 more round-trippers before the 1973 season closed. It meant baseball would not crown its new home-run champion until the following season.

As Aaron was preparing for 1974, his 21st year in the big leagues, he knew the media crush would be more intense than ever, and that it wouldn't subside until the new home-run record was history. "It used to be that nobody bothered me, and I didn't bother anybody. I'd hit three homers, there would be no reporters around. Now they're around every day."

Henry tied Ruth almost before the umpire finished shouting "Play ball!" Jack Billingham of the Cincinnati Reds delivered, and with his first swing of the 1974 season, Aaron smashed the ball over the left-center-field fence. The next one would do it. The only remaining questions were when and where Henry Aaron would hit the record-breaker. Atlanta management announced they were planning to rest Aaron for the next two games in Cincinnati to insure that Henry break the mark before the home-town fans in Atlanta. A big flap ensued, with baseball commissioner Bowie Kuhn sending a stern warning to the Braves that the club would be severely penalized if it did not field its best team—

which of course meant playing Henry Aaron. Atlanta manager Eddie Mathews finally backed down, agreeing to play Hank on Sunday rather than risk the wrath of the commissioner. Hank did not hit a home run.

The Braves returned home. More than 52,000 fans packed into Atlanta Stadium on the cool, damp spring night. The crowd, hoping and waiting to be in on history, exuded a special sort of electricity.

A thunderous ovation shook the park when Aaron strolled to the plate. Al Downing of the Los Angeles Dodgers was on the mound. The little left-hander delivered five pitches to Aaron, only one of them a strike. Hank walked. The bat never left his shoulder. The crowd booed lustily.

Aaron's second turn at bat came in the fourth inning. Tension again gripped the stadium as Henry set himself in the batter's box. Downing's first offering was a change up in the dirt—ball one. The veteran hurler seemed determined not to give Aaron anything good to hit.

Downing toed the rubber. Aaron coiled into his slightly closed stance, bat cocked, extending high over his head. The pitch—a fast ball—came in hard, waist high, over the plate. The date was April 8, 1974 and the time was 9:07 P.M. when Henry Aaron strode into the pitch and swiftly swung his bat. The crack of the bat was pure and solid, and the ball carried far and deep to left center. Dodger outfielders Jimmy Wynn and Bill Buckner converged near the wall, Buckner scaling the wire-mesh fence. He dropped back down. He had no chance. Henry Aaron had